ASIAN COOKBOOK

SUPER TASTY RECIPES MADE SIMPLE

DAVID ZHENG

Table of Contents

Introduction

Everyone who loves to cook, loves to experiment with new dishes and new taste sensations. Chinese cuisine has become immensely popular in recent years because it offers a different range of flavours to enjoy. Most dishes are cooked on top of the stove, and many are quickly prepared and cooked so are ideal for the busy cook who wants to create an appetising and attractive dish when there is little time to spare. If you really enjoy Chinese cooking, you will probably already have a wok, and this is the perfect utensil for cooking most of the dishes in the book. If you have yet to be convinced that this style of cooking is for you, use a good frying pan or saucepan to try out the recipes. When you find how easy they are to prepare and how tasty to eat, you will almost certainly want to invest in a wok for your kitchen.

Marinated Abalone

Serves 4

450 g/1 lb canned abalone

45 ml/3 tbsp soy sauce

30 ml/2 tbsp wine vinegar

5 ml/1 tsp sugar

few drops of sesame oil

Drain the abalone and slice it thinly or cut it into strips. Mix together the remaining ingredients, pour over the abalone and toss well. Cover and refrigerate for 1 hour.

Braised Bamboo Shoots

Serves 4

60 ml/4 tbsp groundnut (peanut) oil
225 g/8 oz bamboo shoots, cut into strips
60 ml/4 tbsp chicken stock
15 ml/1 tbsp soy sauce
5 ml/1 tsp sugar
5 ml/1 tsp rice wine or dry sherry

Heat the oil and stir-fry the bamboo shoots for 3 minutes. Mix the stock, soy sauce, sugar and wine or sherry and add it to the pan. Cover and simmer for 20 minutes. Leave to cool and chill before serving.

Chicken with Cucumber

Serves 4

1 cucumber, peeled and seeded

225 g/8 oz cooked chicken, torn into shreds

5 ml/1 tsp mustard powder

2.5 ml/¬Ω tsp salt

30 ml/2 tbsp wine vinegar

Cut the cucumber into strips and arrange on a flat serving plate. Arrange the chicken on top. Mix together the mustard, salt and wine vinegar and spoon over the chicken just before serving.

Chicken Sesame

Serves 4

350 g/12 oz cooked chicken

120 ml/4 fl oz/¬Ω cup water

5 ml/1 tsp mustard powder

15 ml/1 tbsp sesame seeds

2.5 ml/¬Ω tsp salt

pinch of sugar

45 ml/3 tbsp chopped fresh coriander

5 spring onions (scallions), chopped

¬Ω head lettuce, shredded

Tear the chicken into fine shreds. Mix just enough water into the mustard to make a smooth paste and stir it into the chicken. Toast the sesame seeds in a dry pan until lightly golden then add them to the chicken and sprinkle with salt and sugar. Add half the parsley and the spring onions and toss together thoroughly. Arrange the lettuce on a serving plate, top with the chicken mixture and garnish with the remaining parsley.

Lychees with Ginger

Serves 4

1 large watermelon, halved and seeded

450 g/1 lb canned lychees, drained

5 cm/2 in stem ginger, sliced

few mint leaves

Fill the melon halves with lychees and ginger, decorate with mint leaves. Chill before serving.

Serves 4

8 chicken wings

2 spring onions (scallions), chopped

75 ml/5 tbsp soy sauce

120 ml/4 fl oz/¬Ω cup water

30 ml/2 tbsp brown sugar

Cut off and discard the bony tips of the chicken wings and cut them in half. Place in a pan with the remaining ingredients, bring to the boil, cover and simmer for 30 minutes. Remove the lid and continue to simmer for a further 15 minutes, basting frequently. Leave to cool then chill before serving.

Crab Meat with Cucumber

Serves 4

100 g/4 oz crab meat, flaked

2 cucumbers, peeled and shredded

1 slice ginger root, minced

15 ml/1 tbsp soy sauce

30 ml/2 tbsp wine vinegar

5 ml/1 tsp sugar

few drops of sesame oil

Place the crab meat and cucumbers in a bowl. Mix together the remaining ingredients, pour over the crab meat mixture and toss together well. Cover and refrigerate for 30 minutes before serving.

Marinated Mushrooms

Serves 4

225 g/8 oz button mushrooms

30 ml/2 tbsp soy sauce

15 ml/1 tbsp rice wine or dry sherry

pinch of salt

few drops of tabasco sauce

few drops of sesame oil

Blanch the mushrooms in boiling water for 2 minutes then drain and pat dry. Place in a bowl and pour over the remaining ingredients. Toss together well and chill before serving.

Marinated Garlic Mushrooms

Serves 4

225 g/8 oz button mushrooms

3 cloves garlic, crushed

30 ml/2 tbsp soy sauce

30 ml/2 tbsp rice wine or dry sherry

15 ml/1 tbsp sesame oil

pinch of salt

Place the mushrooms and garlic in a colander, pour over boiling water and leave to stand for 3 minutes. Drain and pat dry thoroughly. Mix together the remaining ingredients, pour the marinade over the mushrooms and leave to marinate for 1 hour.

Prawns and Cauliflower

Serves 4

225 g/8 oz cauliflower florets

100 g/ 4 oz peeled prawns

15 ml/1 tbsp soy sauce

5 ml/1 tsp sesame oil

Part boil the cauliflower for about 5 minutes until tender but still crunchy. Mix with the prawns, sprinkle with soy sauce and sesame oil and toss together. Chill before serving.

Sesame Ham Sticks

Serves 4

225 g/8 oz ham, cut into strips

10 ml/2 tsp soy sauce

2.5 ml/¬Ω tsp sesame oil

Arrange the ham on a serving plate. Mix the soy sauce and sesame oil, sprinkle over the ham and serve.

Cold Tofu

Serves 4

450 g/1 lb tofu, sliced
45 ml/3 tbsp soy sauce
45 ml/3 tbsp groundnut (peanut) oil
freshly ground pepper

Place the tofu, a few slices at a time, in a sieve and plunge into boiling water for 40 seconds then drain and arrange on a serving plate. Leave to cool. Mix together the soy sauce and oil, sprinkle over the tofu and serve sprinkled with pepper.

Chicken with Bacon

Serves 4

225 g/8 oz chicken, very thinly sliced

75 ml/5 tbsp soy sauce

15 ml/1 tbsp rice wine or dry sherry

1 clove garlic, crushed

15 ml/1 tbsp brown sugar

5 ml/1 tsp salt

5 ml/1 tsp minced ginger root

225 g/8 oz lean bacon, cubed

100 g/4 oz water chestnuts, very thinly sliced

30 ml/2 tbsp honey

Place the chicken in a bowl. Mix 45 ml/3 tbsp of soy sauce with the wine or sherry, garlic, sugar, salt and ginger, pour over the chicken and marinate for about 3 hours. Thread the chicken, bacon and chestnuts on to kebab skewers. Mix the remaining soy sauce with the honey and brush over the kebabs. Grill (broil) under a hot grill for about 10 minutes until cooked, turning frequently and brushing with more glaze as they cook.

Chicken and Banana Fries

Serves 4

2 cooked chicken breasts

2 firm bananas

6 slices bread

4 eggs

120 ml/4 fl oz/¬Ω cup milk

50 g/2 oz/¬Ω cup plain (all-purpose) flour

225 g/8 oz/4 cups fresh breadcrumbs

oil for deep-frying

Cut the chicken into 24 pieces. Peel the bananas and cut lengthways into quarters. Cut each quarter into thirds to give 24 pieces. Cut the crusts off the bread and cut it into quarters. Beat the eggs and milk and brush over one side of the bread. Place one piece of chicken and one piece of banana on the egg-coated side of each piece of bread. Coat the squares lightly in flour then dip in egg and coat with breadcrumbs. Dip again into the egg and breadcrumbs. Heat the oil and fry a few squares at a time until golden brown. Drain on kitchen paper before serving.

Chicken with Ginger and Mushrooms

Serves 4

225 g/8 oz chicken breast fillets

5 ml/1 tsp five-spice powder

15 ml/1 tbsp plain (all-purpose) flour

120 ml/4 fl oz/¬Ω cup groundnut (peanut) oil

4 shallots, halved

1 clove garlic, sliced

1 slice ginger root, chopped

25 g/1 oz/¬° cup cashew nuts

5 ml/1 tsp honey

15 ml/1 tbsp rice flour

75 ml/5 tbsp rice wine or dry sherry

100 g/4 oz mushrooms, quartered

2.5 ml/¬Ω tsp turmeric

6 yellow chilli peppers, halved

5 ml/1 tsp soy sauce

juice of ¬Ω lime

salt and pepper

4 crisp lettuce leaves

Cut the chicken breast diagonally across the grain into fine strips. Sprinkle with five-spice powder and coat lightly with flour. Heat 15 ml/1 tbsp oil and stir-fry the chicken until golden brown. Remove from the pan. Heat a little more oil and stir-fry the shallots, garlic, ginger and cashew nuts for 1 minute. Add the honey and stir round until the vegetables are coated. Sprinkle with flour then stir in the wine or sherry. Add the mushrooms, turmeric and chilli peppers and cook for 1 minute. Add the chicken, soy sauce, half the lime juice, salt and pepper and heat through. Remove from the pan and keep warm. Heat a little more oil, add the lettuce leaves and fry quickly, seasoning with salt and pepper and the remaining lime juice. Arrange the lettuce leaves on a warmed serving dish, spread the meat and vegetables on top and serve.

Chicken and Ham

Serves 4

225 g/8 oz chicken, very thinly sliced

75 ml/5 tbsp soy sauce

15 ml/1 tbsp rice wine or dry sherry

15 ml/1 tbsp brown sugar

5 ml/1 tsp minced ginger root

1 clove garlic, crushed

225 g/8 oz cooked ham, cubed

30 ml/2 tbsp honey

Place the chicken in a bowl with 45 ml/3 tbsp of soy sauce, the wine or sherry, sugar, ginger and garlic. Leave to marinate for 3 hours. Thread the chicken and ham on to kebab skewers. Mix the remaining soy sauce with the honey and brush over the kebabs. Grill (broil) under a hot grill for about 10 minutes, turning frequently and brushing with the glaze as they cook.

Grilled Chicken Livers

Serves 4

450 g/1 lb chicken livers

45 ml/3 tbsp soy sauce

15 ml/1 tbsp rice wine or dry sherry

15 ml/1 tbsp brown sugar

5 ml/1 tsp salt

5 ml/1 tsp minced ginger root

1 clove garlic, crushed

Parboil the chicken livers in boiling water for 2 minutes then drain well. Place in a bowl with all the remaining ingredients except the oil and marinate for about 3 hours. Thread the chicken livers on to kebab skewers and grill (broil) under a hot grill for about 8 minutes until golden brown.

Crab Balls with Water Chestnuts

Serves 4

450 g/1 lb crab meat, minced

100 g/4 oz water chestnuts, chopped

1 clove garlic, crushed

1 cm/¬Ω in slice ginger root, minced

45 ml/3 tbsp cornflour (cornstarch)

30 ml/2 tbsp soy sauce

15 ml/1 tbsp rice wine or dry sherry

5 ml/1 tsp salt

5 ml/1 tsp sugar

3 eggs, beaten

oil for deep-frying

Mix together all the ingredients except the oil and shape into small balls. Heat the oil and deep-fry the crab balls until golden brown. Drain well before serving.

Dim Sum

Serves 4

100 g/4 oz peeled prawns, chopped
225 g/8 oz lean pork, finely chopped
50 g/2 oz Chinese cabbage, finely chopped
3 spring onions (scallions), chopped
1 egg, beaten
30 ml/2 tbsp cornflour (cornstarch)
10 ml/2 tsp soy sauce
5 ml/1 tsp sesame oil
5 ml/1 tsp oyster sauce
24 wonton skins
oil for deep-frying

Mix together the prawns, pork, cabbage and spring onions. Mix in the egg, cornflour, soy sauce, sesame oil and oyster sauce. Place spoonfuls of the mixture on to the centre of each wonton skin. Gently press the wrappers around the filling, tucking the edges together but leaving the tops open. Heat the oil and fry the dim sums a few at a time until golden brown. Drain well and serve hot.

Ham and Chicken Rolls

Serves 4

2 chicken breasts

1 clove garlic, crushed

2.5 ml/¬Ω tsp salt

2.5 ml/¬Ω tsp five-spice powder

4 slices cooked ham

1 egg, beaten

30 ml/2 tbsp milk

25 g/1 oz/¬° cup plain (all-purpose) flour

4 egg roll skins

oil for deep-frying

Slice the chicken breasts in half. Pound them until very thin. Mix the garlic, salt and five-spice powder and sprinkle over the chicken. Place a slice of ham on top of each piece of chicken and roll them up tightly. Mix the egg and milk. Coat the chicken pieces lightly with flour then dip in the egg mixture. Place each piece on an egg roll skin and brush the edges with beaten egg. Fold in the sides then roll together, pinching the edges to seal. Heat the oil and fry the rolls for about 5 minutes until golden brown and cooked through. Drain on kitchen paper then cut into thick diagonal slices to serve.

Baked Ham Turnovers

Serves 4

350 g/12 oz/3 cups plain (all-purpose) flour
175 g/6 oz/¬œ cup butter
120 ml/4 fl oz/¬Ω cup water
225 g/8 oz ham, chopped
100 g/4 oz bamboo shoots, chopped
2 spring onions (scallions), chopped
15 ml/1 tbsp soy sauce
30 ml/2 tbsp sesame seeds

Place the flour in a bowl and rub in the butter. Mix in the water to form a dough. Roll out the dough and cut into 5 cm/2 in circles. Mix together all the remaining ingredients except the sesame seeds and place a spoonful on each circle. Brush the edges of the pastry with water and seal together. Brush the outsides with water and sprinkle with sesame seeds. Bake in a preheated oven at 180¬∞C/350¬∞F/gas mark 4 for 30 minutes.

Pseudo Smoked Fish

Serves 4

1 sea bass

3 slices ginger root, sliced

1 clove garlic, crushed

1 spring onion (scallion), thickly sliced

75 ml/5 tbsp soy sauce

30 ml/2 tbsp rice wine or dry sherry

2.5 ml/¬Ω tsp ground anise

2.5 ml/¬Ω tsp sesame oil

10 ml/2 tsp sugar

120 ml/4 fl oz/¬Ω cup stock

oil for deep-frying

5 ml/1 tsp cornflour (cornstarch)

Trim the fish and cut it into 5 mm (¬° in) slices against the grain. Mix together the ginger, garlic, spring onion, 60 ml/4 tbsp of soy sauce, the sherry, anise and sesame oil. Pour over the fish and toss gently. Leave to stand for 2 hours, turning occasionally.

Drain the marinade into a pan and pat the fish dry on kitchen paper. Add the sugar, stock and remaining soy sauce to the marinade, bring to the boil and simmer for 1 minute. If the sauce needs to be thickened, mix the cornflour with a little cold water, stir it into the sauce and simmer, stirring, until the sauce thickens.

Meanwhile, heat the oil and deep-fry the fish until golden brown. Drain well. Dip the pieces of fish in the marinade then arrange them on a warmed serving plate. Serve hot or cold.

Stuffed Mushrooms

Serves 4

12 large dried mushroom caps

225 g/8 oz crab meat

3 water chestnuts, minced

2 spring onions (scallions), finely chopped

1 egg white

15 ml/1 tbsp cornflour (cornstarch)

15 ml/1 tbsp soy sauce

15 ml/1 tbsp rice wine or dry sherry

Soak the mushrooms in warm water overnight. Squeeze dry. Mix together the remaining ingredients and use to fill the mushroom caps. Arrange on a steamer rack and steam for 40 minutes. Serve hot.

Oyster Sauce Mushrooms

Serves 4

10 dried Chinese mushrooms
250 ml/8 fl oz/1 cup beef stock
15 ml/1 tbsp cornflour (cornstarch)
30 ml/2 tbsp oyster sauce
5 ml/1 tsp rice wine or dry sherry

Soak the mushrooms in warm water for 30 minutes then drain, reserving 250 ml/8 fl oz/1 cup of soaking liquid. Discard the stalks. Mix 60 ml/4 tbsp of the beef stock with the cornflour to a paste. Bring the remaining beef stock to the boil with the mushrooms and mushroom liquid, cover and simmer for 20 minutes. Remove the mushrooms from the liquid with a slotted spoon and arrange on a warm serving plate. Add the oyster sauce and sherry to the pan and simmer, stirring for 2 minutes. Stir in the cornflour paste and simmer, stir until the sauce thickens. Pour over the mushrooms and serve at once.

Pork and Lettuce Rolls

Serves 4

4 dried Chinese mushrooms
15 ml/1 tbsp groundnut (peanut) oil
225 g/8 oz lean pork, chopped
100 g/4 oz bamboo shoots, chopped
100 g/4 oz water chestnuts, chopped
4 spring onions (scallions), chopped
175 g/6 oz crab meat, flaked
30 ml/2 tbsp rice wine or dry sherry
15 ml/1 tbsp soy sauce
10 ml/2 tsp oyster sauce
10 ml/2 tsp sesame oil
9 Chinese leaves

Soak the mushrooms in warm water for 30 minutes then drain. Discard the stalks and chop the caps. Heat the oil and stir-fry the pork for 5 minutes. Add the mushrooms, bamboo shoots, water chestnuts, spring onions and crab meat and stir-fry for 2 minutes. Mix the wine or sherry, soy sauce, oyster sauce and sesame oil and stir it into the pan. Remove from the heat. Meanwhile, blanch the Chinese leaves in boiling water for 1 minute then drain. Place spoonfuls of the pork mixture on the centre of each leaf, fold over the sides then roll up to serve.

Pork and Chestnut Meatballs

Serves 4

450 g/1 lb minced (ground) pork

50 g/2 oz mushrooms, finely chopped

50 g/2 oz water chestnuts, finely chopped

1 clove garlic, crushed

1 egg, beaten

30 ml/2 tbsp soy sauce

15 ml/1 tbsp rice wine or dry sherry

5 ml/1 tsp minced ginger root

5 ml/1 tsp sugar

salt

30 ml/2 tbsp cornflour (cornstarch)

oil for deep-frying

Mix together all the ingredients except the cornflour and shape the mixture into small balls. Roll in the cornflour. Heat the oil and deep-fry the meatballs for about 10 minutes until golden brown. Drain well before serving.

Pork Dumplings

Serves 4‚Äì6

450 g/1 lb plain (all-purpose) flour

500 ml/17 fl oz/2 cups water

450 g/1 lb cooked pork, minced

225 g/8 oz peeled prawns, chopped

4 stalks celery, chopped

15 ml/1 tbsp soy sauce

15 ml/1 tbsp rice wine or dry sherry

15 ml/1 tbsp sesame oil

5 ml/1 tsp salt

2 spring onions (scallions), finely chopped

2 cloves garlic, crushed

1 slice ginger root, minced

Mix together the flour and water to a soft dough and knead well. Cover and leave to stand for 10 minutes. Roll out the dough as thinly as possible and cut into 5 cm/2 in circles. Mix together all the remaining ingredients. Place spoonfuls of the mixture on each circle, dampen the edges and seal into a semi-circle. Bring a saucepan of water to the boil then gently place the dumplings in the water.

Pork and Veal Rissoles

Serves 4

100 g/4 oz minced (ground) pork

100 g/4 oz minced (ground) veal

1 slice streaky bacon, minced (ground)

15 ml/1 tbsp soy sauce

salt and pepper

1 egg, beaten

30 ml/2 tbsp cornflour (cornstarch)

oil for deep-frying

Mix together the minced meats and bacon and season with salt and pepper. Bind together with the egg, shape into walnut-sized balls and dust with cornflour. Heat the oil and deep-fry until golden brown. Drain well before serving.

Butterfly Prawns

Serves 4

450 g/1 lb large peeled prawns
15 ml/1 tbsp soy sauce
5 ml/1 tsp rice wine or dry sherry
5 ml/1 tsp minced ginger root
2.5 ml/¬Ω tsp salt
2 eggs, beaten
30 ml/2 tbsp cornflour (cornstarch)
15 ml/1 tbsp plain (all-purpose) flour
oil for deep-frying

Slice the prawns halfway through the back and spread them out to form a butterfly shape. Mix together the soy sauce, wine or sherry, ginger and salt. Pour over the prawns and leave to marinate for 30 minutes. Remove from the marinade and pat dry. Beat the egg with the cornflour and flour to a batter and dip the prawns in the batter. Heat the oil and deep-fry the prawns until golden brown. Drain well before serving.

Chinese Prawns

Serves 4

450 g/1 lb unpeeled prawns
30 ml/2 tbsp Worcestershire sauce
15 ml/1 tbsp soy sauce
15 ml/1 tbsp rice wine or dry sherry
15 ml/1 tbsp brown sugar

Place the prawns in a bowl. Mix together the remaining ingredients, pour over the prawns and leave to marinate for 30 minutes. Transfer to a baking tin and bake in a preheated oven at 150¬∞C/300¬∞F/ gas mark 2 for 25 minutes. Serve hot or cold in the shells for the guests to shell their own.

Prawn Crackers

Serves 4

100 g/4 oz prawn crackers
oil for deep-frying

Heat the oil until very hot. Add a handful of prawn crackers at a time and fry for a few seconds until they have puffed up. Remove from the oil and drain on kitchen paper while you continue to fry the crackers.

Crispy Prawns

Serves 4

450 g/1 lb peeled tiger prawns
15 ml/1 tbsp rice wine or dry sherry
10 ml/2 tsp soy sauce
5 ml/1 tsp five-spice powder
salt and pepper
90 ml/6 tbsp cornflour (cornstarch)
2 eggs, beaten
100 g/4 oz breadcrumbs
groundnut oil for deep-frying

Mix the prawns with the wine or sherry, soy sauce and five-spice powder and season with salt and pepper. Toss them in the cornflour then coat in beaten egg and breadcrumbs. Deep-fry in hot oil for a few minutes until lightly browned then drain and serve at once.

Prawns with Ginger Sauce

Serves 4

15 ml/1 tbsp soy sauce

5 ml/1 tsp rice wine or dry sherry

5 ml/1 tsp sesame oil

450 g/1 lb peeled prawns

30 ml/2 tbsp chopped fresh parsley

15 ml/1 tbsp wine vinegar

5 ml/1 tsp chopped ginger root

Mix together the soy sauce, wine or sherry and sesame oil. Pour over the prawns, cover and leave to marinate for 30 minutes. Grill the prawns for a few minutes until just cooked, basting with the marinade. Meanwhile, mix together the parsley, wine vinegar and ginger to serve with the prawns.

Prawn and Noodle Rolls

Serves 4

50 g/2 oz egg noodles, broken into pieces
15 ml/1 tbsp groundnut (peanut) oil
50 g/2 oz lean pork, finely chopped
100 g/4 oz mushrooms, chopped
3 spring onions (scallions), chopped
100 g/4 oz peeled prawns, chopped
15 ml/1 tbsp rice wine or dry sherry
salt and pepper
24 wonton skins
1 egg, beaten
oil for deep-frying

Cook the noodles in boiling water for 5 minutes then drain and chop. Heat the oil and stir-fry the pork for 4 minutes. Add the mushrooms and onions and stir-fry for 2 minutes then remove from the heat. Mix in the prawns, wine or sherry and noodles and season to taste with salt and pepper. Place spoonfuls of the mixture on the centre of each wonton skin and brush the edges with beaten egg. Fold over the edges then roll up the wrappers, sealing the edges together. Heat the oil and deep-fry the rolls a few at a time for about 5 minutes until golden. Drain on kitchen paper before serving.

Prawn Toasts

Serves 4

2 eggs 450 g/1 lb peeled prawns, minced

15 ml/1 tbsp cornflour (cornstarch)

1 onion, finely chopped

30 ml/2 tbsp soy sauce

15 ml/1 tbsp rice wine or dry sherry

5 ml/1 tsp salt

5 ml/1 tsp minced ginger root

8 slices bread, cut into triangles

oil for deep-frying

Mix together 1 egg with all the remaining ingredients except the bread and oil. Spoon the mixture on to the bread triangles and press into a dome. Brush with the remaining egg. Heat about 5 cm/2 in of oil and deep-fry the bread triangles until golden brown. Drain well before serving.

Pork and Prawn Wontons with Sweet and Sour Sauce

Serves 4

120 ml/4 fl oz/¬Ω cup water

60 ml/4 tbsp wine vinegar

60 ml/4 tbsp brown sugar

30 ml/2 tbsp tomato pur√©e (paste)

10 ml/2 tsp cornflour (cornstarch)

25 g/1 oz mushrooms, chopped

25 g/1 oz peeled prawns, chopped

50 g/2 oz lean pork, chopped

2 spring onions (scallions), chopped

5 ml/1 tsp soy sauce

2.5 ml/¬Ω tsp grated ginger root

1 clove garlic, crushed

24 wonton skins

oil for deep-frying

Mix together the water, wine vinegar, sugar, tomato pur√©e and cornflour in a small saucepan. Bring to the boil, stirring continuously, then simmer for 1 minute. Remove from the heat and keep warm.

Mix the mushrooms, prawns, pork, spring onions, soy sauce, ginger and garlic. Place spoonfuls of the filling on each skin, brush the edges with water and press together to seal. Heat the oil and deep-fry the wontons a few at a time until golden brown. Drain on kitchen paper and serve hot with sweet and sour sauce.

Chicken Stock

Makes 2 litres/3½ pts/8½ cups

1.5 kg/2 lb cooked or raw bones of chicken

450 g/1 lb pork bones

1 cm/½ in piece ginger root

3 spring onions (scallions), sliced

1 clove garlic, crushed

5 ml/1 tsp salt

2.25 litres/4 pts/10 cups water

Bring all the ingredients to the boil, cover and simmer for 15 minutes. Skim off any fat. Cover and simmer for 1½ hours. Strain, cool and skim. Freeze in small quantities or keep refrigerated and use within 2 days.

Bean Sprout and Pork Soup

Serves 4

450 g/1 lb pork, cubed

1.5 l/2½ pts/6 cups chicken stock

5 slices ginger root

350 g/12 oz bean sprouts

15 ml/1 tbsp salt

Blanch the pork in boiling water for 10 minutes then drain. Bring the stock to the boil and add the pork and ginger. Cover and simmer for 50 minutes. Add the bean sprouts and salt and simmer for 20 minutes.

Abalone and Mushroom Soup

Serves 4

60 ml/4 tbsp groundnut (peanut) oil

100 g/4 oz lean pork, cut into strips

225 g/8 oz canned abalone, cut into strips

100 g/4 oz mushrooms, sliced

2 stalks celery, sliced

50 g/2 oz ham, cut into strips

2 onions, sliced

1.5 l/2½ pts/6 cups water

30 ml/2 tbsp wine vinegar

45 ml/3 tbsp soy sauce

2 slices ginger root, chopped

salt and freshly ground pepper

15 ml/1 tbsp cornflour (cornstarch)

45 ml/3 tbsp water

Heat the oil and fry the pork, abalone, mushrooms, celery, ham and onions for 8 minutes. Add the water and wine vinegar, bring to the boil, cover and simmer for 20 minutes. Add the soy sauce, ginger, salt and pepper. Blend the cornflour to a paste with the water, stir it into the soup and simmer, stirring, for 5 minutes until the soup clears and thickens.

Chicken and Asparagus Soup

Serves 4

100 g/4 oz chicken, shredded

2 egg whites

2.5 ml/½ tsp salt

30 ml/2 tbsp cornflour (cornstarch)

225 g/8 oz asparagus, cut into 5 cm/2 in chunks

100 g/4 oz bean sprouts

1.5 l/2½ pts/6 cups chicken stock

100 g/4 oz button mushrooms

Mix the chicken with the egg whites, salt and cornflour and leave to stand for 30 minutes. Cook the chicken in boiling water for about 10 minutes until cooked through then drain well. Blanch the asparagus in boiling water for 2 minutes then drain. Blanch the bean sprouts in boiling water for 3 minutes then drain. Pour the stock into a large pan and add the chicken, asparagus, mushrooms and bean sprouts. Bring to the boil and season to taste with salt. Simmer for a few minutes to allow the flavours to develop and until the vegetables are tender but still crisp.

Beef Soup

Serves 4

225 g/8 oz minced (ground) beef

15 ml/1 tbsp soy sauce

15 ml/1 tbsp rice wine or dry sherry

15 ml/1 tbsp cornflour (cornstarch)

1.2 l/2 pts/5 cups chicken stock

5 ml/1 tsp chilli bean sauce

salt and pepper

2 eggs, beaten

6 spring onions (scallions), chopped

Mix the beef with the soy sauce, wine or sherry and cornflour. Add to the stock and gradually bring to the boil, stirring. Add the chilli bean sauce and season to taste with salt and pepper, cover and simmer for about 10 minutes, stirring occasionally. Stir in the eggs and serve sprinkled with the spring onions.

Beef and Chinese Leaves Soup

Serves 4

200 g/7 oz lean beef, cut into strips
15 ml/1 tbsp soy sauce
15 ml/1 tbsp groundnut (peanut) oil
1.5 l/2½ pts/6 cups beef stock
5 ml/1 tsp salt
2.5 ml/½ tsp sugar
½ head Chinese leaves, cut into chunks

Mix the beef with the soy sauce and oil and leave to marinate for 30 minutes, stirring occasionally. Bring the stock to the boil with the salt and sugar, add the Chinese leaves and simmer for about 10 minutes until almost cooked. Add the beef and simmer for a further 5 minutes.

Cabbage Soup

Serves 4

60 ml/4 tbsp groundnut (peanut) oil
2 onions, chopped
100 g/4 oz lean pork, cut into strips
225 g/8 oz Chinese cabbage, shredded
10 ml/2 tsp sugar
1.2 l/2 pts/5 cups chicken stock
45 ml/3 tbsp soy sauce
salt and pepper
15 ml/1 tbsp cornflour (cornstarch)

Heat the oil and fry the onions and pork until lightly browned. Add the cabbage and sugar and stir-fry for 5 minutes. Add the stock and soy sauce and season to taste with salt and pepper. Bring to the boil, cover and simmer gently for 20 minutes. Mix the cornflour with a little water, stir it into the soup and simmer, stirring, until the soup thickens and clears.

Piquant Beef Soup

Serves 4

45 ml/3 tbsp groundnut (peanut) oil

1 clove garlic, crushed

5 ml/1 tsp salt

225 g/8 oz minced (ground) beef

6 spring onions (scallions), cut into strips

1 red pepper, cut into strips

1 green pepper, cut into strips

225 g/8 oz cabbage, shredded

1 l/1¾ pts/4¼ cups beef stock

30 ml/2 tbsp plum sauce

30 ml/2 tbsp hoisin sauce

45 ml/3 tbsp soy sauce

2 pieces stem ginger, chopped

2 eggs

5 ml/1 tsp sesame oil

225 g/8 oz transparent noodles, soaked

Heat the oil and fry the garlic and salt until lightly browned. Add the beef and brown quickly. Add the vegetables and stir-fry until translucent. Add the stock, plum sauce, hoisin sauce, 30 ml/2 tbsp of soy sauce and the ginger, bring to the boil and simmer for 10 minutes. Beat the eggs with the sesame oil and remaining soy sauce. Add to the soup with the noodles and cook, stirring, until the eggs form strands and the noodles are tender.

Celestial Soup

Serves 4

2 spring onions (scallions), minced

1 clove garlic, crushed

30 ml/2 tbsp chopped fresh parsley

5 ml/1 tsp salt

15 ml/1 tbsp groundnut (peanut) oil

30 ml/2 tbsp soy sauce

1.5 l/2½ pts/6 cups water

Mix together the spring onions, garlic, parsley, salt, oil and soy sauce. Bring to the water to the boil, pour over the spring onion mixture and leave to stand for 3 minutes.

Chicken and Bamboo Shoot Soup

Serves 4

2 chicken legs

30 ml/2 tbsp groundnut (peanut) oil

5 ml/1 tsp rice wine or dry sherry

1.5 l/2½ pts/6 cups chicken stock

3 spring onions, sliced

100 g/4 oz bamboo shoots, cut into chunks

5 ml/1 tsp minced ginger root

salt

Bone the chicken and cut the flesh into chunks. Heat the oil and fry the chicken until sealed on all sides. Add the stock, spring onions, bamboo shoots and ginger, bring to the boil and simmer for about 20 minutes until the chicken is tender. Season to taste with salt before serving.

Chicken and Corn Soup

Serves 4

1 l/1¾ pts/4¼ cups chicken stock

100 g/4 oz chicken, minced

200 g/7 oz creamed sweetcorn

slice ham, chopped

eggs, beaten

15 ml/1 tbsp rice wine or dry sherry

Bring the stock and chicken to the boil, cover and simmer for 15 minutes. Add the sweetcorn and ham, cover and simmer for 5 minutes. Add the eggs and sherry, stirring slowly with a chopstick so that the eggs form into threads. Remove from the heat, cover and leave to stand for 3 minutes before serving.

Chicken and Ginger Soup

Serves 4

4 dried Chinese mushrooms

1.5 l/2½ pts/6 cups water or chicken stock

225 g/8 oz chicken meat, cubed

10 slices ginger root

5 ml/1 tsp rice wine or dry sherry

salt

Soak the mushrooms in warm water for 30 minutes then drain. Discard the stalks. Bring the water or stock to the boil with the remaining ingredients and simmer gently for about 20 minutes until the chicken is cooked.

Chicken Soup with Chinese Mushrooms

Serves 4

25 g/1 oz dried Chinese mushrooms
100 g/4 oz chicken, shredded
50 g/2 oz bamboo shoots, shredded
30 ml/2 tbsp soy sauce
30 ml/2 tbsp rice wine or dry sherry
1.2 l/2 pts/5 cups chicken stock

Soak the mushrooms in warm water for 30 minutes then drain. Discard the stems and slice the caps. Blanch the mushrooms, chicken and bamboo shoots in boiling water for 30 seconds then drain. Place them in a bowl and stir in the soy sauce and wine or sherry. Leave to marinate for 1 hour. Bring the stock to the boil add the chicken mixture and the marinade. Stir well and simmer for a few minutes until the chicken is thoroughly cooked.

Chicken and Rice Soup

Serves 4

1 l/1¾ pts/4¼ cups chicken stock

225 g/8 oz/1 cup cooked long-grain rice

100 g/4 oz cooked chicken, cut into strips

1 onion, cut into wedges

5 ml/1 tsp soy sauce

Heat all the ingredients together gently until hot without allowing the soup to boil.

Chicken and Coconut Soup

Serves 4

350 g/12 oz chicken breast

salt

10 ml/2 tsp cornflour (cornstarch)

30 ml/2 tbsp groundnut (peanut) oil

1 green chilli pepper, chopped

1 l/1¾ pts/4¼ cups coconut milk

5 ml/1 tsp grated lemon rind

12 lychees

pinch of grated nutmeg

salt and freshly ground pepper

2 lemon balm leaves

Cut the chicken breast diagonally across the grain into strips. Sprinkle with salt and coat with cornflour. Heat 10 ml/2 tsp of oil in a wok, swirl round and pour it out. Repeat once more. Heat the remaining oil and stir-fry the chicken and chilli pepper for 1 minute. Add the coconut milk and bring to the boil. Add the lemon rind and simmer for 5 minutes. Add the lychees, season with nutmeg, salt and pepper and serve garnished with lemon balm.

Clam Soup

Serves 4

2 dried Chinese mushrooms
12 clams, soaked and scrubbed
1.5 l/2½ pts/6 cups chicken stock
50 g/2 oz bamboo shoots, shredded
50 g/2 oz mangetout (snow peas),halved
2 spring onions (scallions), cut into rings
15 ml/1 tbsp rice wine or dry sherry
pinch of freshly ground pepper

Soak the mushrooms in warm water for 30 minutes then drain. Discard the stalks and halve the caps. Steam the clams for about 5 minutes until they open; discard any that remain closed. Remove the clams from their shells. Bring the stock to the boil and add the mushrooms, bamboo shoots, mangetout and spring onions. Simmer, uncovered, for 2 minutes. Add the clams, wine or sherry and pepper and simmer until heated through.

Egg Soup

Serves 4

1.2 l/2 pts/5 cups chicken stock

3 eggs, beaten

45 ml/3 tbsp soy sauce

salt and freshly ground pepper

4 spring onions (scallions), sliced

Bring the stock to the boil. Gradually whisk in the beaten eggs so that they separate into strands. Stir in the soy sauce and season to taste with salt and pepper. Serve garnished with spring onions.

Crab and Scallop Soup

Serves 4

4 dried Chinese mushrooms

15 ml/1 tbsp groundnut (peanut) oil

1 egg, beaten

1.5 l/2½ pts/6 cups chicken stock

175 g/6 oz crab meat, flaked

100 g/4 oz shelled scallops, sliced

100 g/4 oz bamboo shoots, sliced

2 spring onions (scallions), chopped

1 slice ginger root, minced

a few cooked, peeled prawns (optional)

45 ml/3 tbsp cornflour (cornstarch)

90 ml/6 tbsp water

30 ml/2 tbsp rice wine or dry sherry

20 ml/4 tsp soy sauce

2 egg whites

Soak the mushrooms in warm water for 30 minutes then drain. Discard the stalks and slice the caps thinly. Heat the oil, add the egg and tilt the pan so that the egg covers the bottom. Cook until set then turn and cook the other side. Remove from the pan, roll up and cut into thin strips.

Bring the stock to the boil, add the mushrooms, egg strips, crab meat, scallops, bamboo shoots, spring onions, ginger and prawns, if using. Bring back to the boil. Mix the cornflour with 60 ml/4 tbsp of water, the wine or sherry and soy sauce and stir into soup. Simmer, stirring until the soup thickens. Beat the egg whites with the remaining water and drizzle the mixture slowly into the soup, stirring vigorously.

Crab Soup

Serves 4

90 ml/6 tbsp groundnut (peanut) oil

3 onions, chopped

225 g/8 oz white and brown crab meat

1 slice ginger root, minced

1.2 l/2 pts/5 cups chicken stock

150 ml/¼pt/ cup rice wine or dry sherry

45 ml/3 tbsp soy sauce

salt and freshly ground pepper

Heat the oil and fry the onions until soft but not browned. Add the crab meat and ginger and stir-fry for 5 minutes. Add the stock, wine or sherry and soy sauce, season with salt and pepper. Bring to the boil then simmer for 5 minutes.

Fish Soup

Serves 4

225 g/8 oz fish fillets

1 slice ginger root, minced

15 ml/1 tbsp rice wine or dry sherry

30 ml/2 tbsp groundnut (peanut) oil

1.5 l/2½ pts/6 cups fish stock

Cut the fish into thin strips against the grain. Mix the ginger, wine or sherry and oil, add the fish and toss gently. Leave to marinate for 30 minutes, turning occasionally. Bring the stock to the boil, add the fish and simmer gently for 3 minutes.

Fish and Lettuce Soup

Serves 4

225 g/8 oz white fish fillets

30 ml/2 tbsp plain (all-purpose) flour

salt and freshly ground pepper

90 ml/6 tbsp groundnut (peanut) oil

6 spring onions (scallions), sliced

100 g/4 oz lettuce, shredded

1.2 l/2 pts/5 cups water

10 ml/2 tsp finely chopped ginger root

150 ml/¼ pt/generous ½ cup rice wine or dry sherry

30 ml/2 tbsp cornflour (cornstarch)

30 ml/2 tbsp chopped fresh parsley

10 ml/2 tsp lemon juice

30 ml/2 tbsp soy sauce

Cut the fish into thin strips then toss in seasoned flour. Heat the oil and fry the spring onions until soft. Add the lettuce and fry for 2 minutes. Add the fish and cook for 4 minutes. Add the water, ginger and wine or sherry, bring to the boil, cover and simmer for 5 minutes. Mix the cornflour with a little water then stir it into the soup. Simmer, stirring for a further 4 minutes until the soup clears then season with salt and pepper. Serve sprinkled with parsley, lemon juice and soy sauce.

Ginger Soup with Dumplings

Serves 4

5 cm/2 in piece ginger root, grated

350 g/12 oz brown sugar

1.5 l/2½ pts/7 cups water

225 g/8 oz/2 cups rice flour

2.5 ml/½ tsp salt

60 ml/4 tbsp water

Place the ginger, sugar and water in a pan and bring to the boil, stirring. Cover and simmer for about 20 minutes. Strain the soup and return it to the pan.

Meanwhile, place the flour and salt in a bowl and gradually knead in just enough water to make a thick dough. Roll it into small balls and drop the dumplings into the soup. Return the soup to the boil, cover and simmer for a further 6 minutes until the dumplings are cooked.

Hot and Sour Soup

Serves 4

8 dried Chinese mushrooms
1 l/1¾ pts/4¼ cups chicken stock
100 g/4 oz chicken, cut into strips
100 g/4 oz bamboo shoots, cut into strips
100 g/4 oz tofu, cut into strips
15 ml/1 tbsp soy sauce
30 ml/2 tbsp wine vinegar
30 ml/2 tbsp cornflour (cornstarch)
2 eggs, beaten
a few drops sesame oil

Soak the mushrooms in warm water for 30 minutes then drain. Discard the stems and cut the caps into strips. Bring the mushrooms, stock, chicken, bamboo shoots and tofu to the boil, cover and simmer for 10 minutes. Mix the soy sauce, wine vinegar and cornflour to a smooth paste, stir it into the soup and simmer for 2 minutes until the soup is translucent. Slowly add the eggs and sesame oil, stirring with a chopstick. Cover and leave to stand for 2 minutes before serving.

Mushroom Soup

Serves 4

15 dried Chinese mushrooms
1.5 l/2½ pts/6 cups chicken stock
5 ml/1 tsp salt

Soak the mushrooms in warm water for 30 minutes then drain, reserving the liquid. Discard the stalks and cut the caps in half if large and place in a large heatproof bowl. Stand the bowl on a rack in a steamer. Bring the stock to the boil, pour over the mushrooms then cover and steam for 1 hour over gently simmering water. Season to taste with salt and serve.

Mushroom and Cabbage Soup

Serves 4

25 g/1 oz dried Chinese mushrooms

15 ml/1 tbsp groundnut (peanut) oil

50 g/2 oz Chinese leaves, shredded

15 ml/1 tbsp rice wine or dry sherry

15 ml/1 tbsp soy sauce

1.2 l/2 pts/5 cups chicken or vegetable stock

salt and freshly ground pepper

5 ml/1 tsp sesame oil

Soak the mushrooms in warm water for 30 minutes then drain. Discard the stems and slice the caps. Heat the oil and stir-fry the mushrooms and Chinese leaves for 2 minutes until well coated. Stir in the wine or sherry and soy sauce then add the stock. Bring to the boil, season to taste with salt and pepper then simmer for 5 minutes. Sprinkle with sesame oil before serving.

Mushroom Egg Drop Soup

Serves 4

1 l/1¾ pts/4¼ cups chicken stock

30 ml/2 tbsp cornflour (cornstarch)

100 g/4 oz mushrooms, sliced

1 slice onion, finely chopped

pinch of salt

3 drops sesame oil

2.5 ml/½ tsp soy sauce

1 egg, beaten

Mix a little stock with the cornflour then blend together all the ingredients except the egg. Bring to the boil, cover and simmer for 5 minutes. Add the egg, stirring with a chopstick so that the egg forms into threads. Remove from the heat and leave to stand for 2 minutes before serving.

Mushroom and Water Chestnut Soup

Serves 4

1 l/1¾ pts/4¼ cups vegetable stock or water

2 onions, finely chopped

5 ml/1 tsp rice wine or dry sherry

30 ml/2 tbsp soy sauce

225 g/8 oz button mushrooms

100 g/4 oz water chestnuts, sliced

100 g/4 oz bamboo shoots, sliced

few drops of sesame oil

2 lettuce leaves, cut into pieces

2 spring onions (scallions), cut into pieces

Bring the water, onions, wine or sherry and soy sauce to the boil, cover and simmer for 10 minutes. Add the mushrooms, water chestnuts and bamboo shoots, cover and simmer for 5 minutes. Stir in the sesame oil, lettuce leaves and spring onions, remove from the heat, cover and leave to stand for 1 minute before serving.

Pork and Mushroom Soup

Serves 4

60 ml/4 tbsp groundnut (peanut) oil

1 clove garlic, crushed

2 onions, sliced

225 g/8 oz lean pork, cut into strips

1 stick celery, chopped

50 g/2 oz mushrooms, sliced

2 carrots, sliced

1.2 l/2 pts/5 cups beef stock

15 ml/1 tbsp soy sauce

salt and freshly ground pepper

15 ml/1 tbsp cornflour (cornstarch)

Heat the oil and fry the garlic, onions and pork until the onions are soft and lightly browned. Add the celery, mushrooms and carrots, cover and simmer gently for 10 minutes. Bring the stock to the boil then add it to the pan with the soy sauce and season to taste with salt and pepper. Mix the cornflour with a little water then stir it into the pan and simmer, stirring, for about 5 minutes.

Pork and Watercress Soup

Serves 4

1.5 l/2½ pts/6 cups chicken stock

100 g/4 oz lean pork, cut into strips

3 stalks celery, diagonally sliced

2 spring onions (scallions), sliced

1 bunch watercress

5 ml/1 tsp salt

Bring the stock to the boil, add the pork and celery, cover and simmer for 15 minutes. Add the spring onions, watercress and salt and simmer, uncovered, for about 4 minutes.

Pork and Cucumber Soup

Serves 4

100 g/4 oz lean pork, thinly sliced

5 ml/1 tsp cornflour (cornstarch)

15 ml/1 tbsp soy sauce

15 ml/1 tbsp rice wine or dry sherry

1 cucumber

1.5 l/2½ pts/6 cups chicken stock

5 ml/1 tsp salt

Mix together the pork, cornflour, soy sauce and wine or sherry. Toss to coat the pork. Peel the cucumber and cut it in half lengthways then scoop out the seeds. Slice thickly. Bring the stock to the boil, add the pork, cover and simmer for 10 minutes. Stir in the cucumber and simmer for a few minutes until translucent. Stir in the salt and add a little more soy sauce, if liked.

Soup with Porkballs and Noodles

Serves 4

50 g/2 oz rice noodles

225 g/8 oz minced (ground) pork

5 ml/1 tsp cornflour (cornstarch)

2.5 ml/½ tsp salt

30 ml/2 tbsp water

1.5 l/2½ pts/6 cups chicken stock

1 spring onion (scallion), finely chopped

5 ml/1 tsp soy sauce

Place the noodles in cold water to soak while you prepare the meatballs. Mix together the pork, cornflour, a little salt and the water and shape into walnut-sized balls. Bring a saucepan of water to a rolling boil, drop in the pork balls, cover and simmer for 5 minutes. Drain well and drain the noodles. Bring the stock to the boil, add the pork balls and noodles, cover and simmer for 5 minutes. Add the spring onion, soy sauce and remaining salt and simmer for a further 2 minutes.

Spinach and Tofu Soup

Serves 4

1.2 l/2 pts/5 cups chicken stock

200 g/7 oz canned tomatoes, drained and chopped

225 g/8 oz tofu, cubed

225 g/8 oz spinach, chopped

30 ml/2 tbsp soy sauce

5 ml/1 tsp brown sugar

salt and freshly ground pepper

Bring the stock to the boil then add the tomatoes, tofu and spinach and stir gently. Return to the boil and simmer for 5 minutes. Add the soy sauce and sugar and season to taste with salt and pepper. Simmer for 1 minute before serving.

Sweetcorn and Crab Soup

Serves 4

1.2 1/2 pts/5 cups chicken stock

200 g/7 oz sweetcorn

salt and freshly ground pepper

1 egg, beaten

200 g/7 oz crab meat, flaked

3 shallots, chopped

Bring the stock to the boil, add the sweetcorn season with salt and pepper. Simmer for 5 minutes. Just before serving, pour the eggs through a fork and swirl on top of the soup. Serve sprinkled with crab meat and chopped shallots.

Szechuan Soup

Serves 4

4 dried Chinese mushrooms

1.5 l/2½ pts/6 cups chicken stock

75 ml/5 tbsp dry white wine

15 ml/1 tbsp soy sauce

2.5 ml/½ tsp chilli sauce

30 ml/2 tbsp cornflour (cornstarch)

60 ml/4 tbsp water

100 g/4 oz lean pork, cut into strips

50 g/2 oz cooked ham, cut into strips

1 red pepper, cut into strips

50 g/2 oz water chestnuts, sliced

10 ml/2 tsp wine vinegar

5 ml/1 tsp sesame oil

1 egg, beaten

100 g/4 oz peeled prawns

6 spring onions (scallions), chopped

175 g/6 oz tofu, cubed

Soak the mushrooms in warm water for 30 minutes then drain.
Discard the stalks and slice the caps. Bring the stock, wine, soy

sauce and chilli sauce to the boil, cover and simmer for 5 minutes. Blend the cornflour with half the water and stir it into the soup, stirring until the soup thickens. Add the mushrooms, pork, ham, pepper and water chestnuts and simmer for 5 minutes. Stir in the wine vinegar and sesame oil. Beat the egg with the remaining water and drizzle this into the soup, stirring vigorously. Add the prawns, spring onions and tofu and simmer for a few minutes to heat through.

Tofu Soup

Serves 4

1.5 l/2½ pts/6 cups chicken stock

225 g/8 oz tofu, cubed

5 ml/1 tsp salt

5 ml/1 tsp soy sauce

Bring the stock to the boil and add the tofu, salt and soy sauce.
Simmer for a few minutes until the tofu is heated through.

Tofu and Fish Soup

Serves 4

225 g/8 oz white fish fillets, cut into strips

150 ml/¼ pt/generous ½ cup rice wine or dry sherry

10 ml/2 tsp finely minced ginger root

45 ml/3 tbsp soy sauce

2.5 ml/½ tsp salt

60 ml/4 tbsp groundnut (peanut) oil

2 onions, chopped

100 g/4 oz mushrooms, sliced

1.2 l/2 pts/5 cups chicken stock

100 g/4 oz tofu, cubed

salt and freshly ground pepper

Place the fish in a bowl. Mix together the wine or sherry, ginger, soy sauce and salt and pour over the fish. Leave to marinate for 30 minutes. Heat the oil and fry the onion for 2 minutes. Add the mushrooms and continue to fry until the onions are soft but not browned. Add the fish and marinade, bring to the boil, cover and simmer for 5 minutes. Add the stock, bring back to the boil, cover and simmer for 15 minutes. Add the tofu and season to taste with salt and pepper. Simmer until the tofu is cooked.

Tomato Soup

Serves 4

400 g/14 oz canned tomatoes, drained and chopped

1.2 l/2 pts/5 cups chicken stock

1 slice ginger root, minced

15 ml/1 tbsp soy sauce

15 ml/1 tbsp chilli bean sauce

10 ml/2 tsp sugar

Place all the ingredients in a pan and bring slowly to the boil, stirring occasionally. Simmer for about 10 minutes before serving.

Tomato and Spinach Soup

Serves 4

1.2 1/2 pts/5 cups chicken stock

225 g/8 oz canned chopped tomatoes

225 g/8 oz tofu, cubed

225 g/8 oz spinach

30 ml/2 tbsp soy sauce

salt and freshly ground pepper

2.5 ml/½ tsp sugar

2.5 ml/½ tsp rice wine or dry sherry

Bring the stock to the boil then add the tomatoes, tofu and spinach and simmer for 2 minutes. Add the remaining ingredients and simmer for 2 minutes then stir well and serve.

Turnip Soup

Serves 4

1 l/1¾ pts/4¼ cups chicken stock
1 large turnip, thinly sliced
200 g/7 oz lean pork, thinly sliced
15 ml/1 tbsp soy sauce
60 ml/4 tbsp brandy
salt and freshly ground pepper
4 shallots, finely chopped

Bring the stock to the boil, add the turnip and pork, cover and simmer for 20 minutes until the turnip is tender and the meat cooked. Stir in the soy sauce and brandy season to taste. Simmer until hot serve sprinkled with shallots.

Vegetable Soup

Serves 4

6 dried Chinese mushrooms

1 l/1¾ pts/4¼ cups vegetable stock

50 g/2 oz bamboo shoots, cut into strips

50 g/2 oz water chestnuts, sliced

8 mangetout (snow peas), sliced

5 ml/1 tsp soy sauce

Soak the mushrooms in warm water for 30 minutes then drain. Discard the stems and cut the caps into strips. Add them to the stock with the bamboo shoots and water chestnuts and bring to the boil, cover and simmer for 10 minutes. Add the mangetout and soy sauce, cover and simmer for 2 minutes. Leave to stand for 2 minutes before serving.

Vegetarian Soup

Serves 4

¼ white cabbage

2 carrots

3 stalks celery

2 spring onions (scallions)

30 ml/2 tbsp groundnut (peanut) oil

1.5 l/2½ pts/6 cups water

15 ml/1 tbsp soy sauce

15 ml/1 tbsp rice wine or dry sherry

5 ml/1 tsp salt

freshly ground pepper

Cut the vegetables into strips. Heat the oil and fry the vegetables for 2 minutes until they begin to soften. Add the remaining ingredients, bring to the boil, cover and simmer for 15 minutes.

Watercress Soup

Serves 4

1 l/1¾ pts/4¼ cups chicken stock
1 onion, finely chopped
1 stick celery, finely chopped
225 g/8 oz watercress, roughly chopped
salt and freshly ground pepper

Bring the stock, onion and celery to the boil, cover and simmer for 15 minutes. Add the watercress, cover and simmer for 5 minutes. Season with salt and pepper.

Deep-Fried Fish with Vegetables

Serves 4

4 dried Chinese mushrooms

4 whole fish, cleaned and scaled

oil for deep-frying

30 ml/2 tbsp cornflour (cornstarch)

45 ml/3 tbsp groundnut (peanut) oil

100 g/4 oz bamboo shoots, cut into strips

50 g/2 oz water chestnuts, cut into strips

50 g/2 oz Chinese cabbage, shredded

2 slices ginger root, minced

30 ml/2 tbsp rice wine or dry sherry

30 ml/2 tbsp water

15 ml/1 tbsp soy sauce

5 ml/1 tsp sugar

120 ml/4 fl oz/¬Ω cup fish stock

salt and freshly ground pepper

¬Ω head lettuce, shredded

15 ml/1 tbsp chopped flat-leaved parsley

Soak the mushrooms in warm water for 30 minutes then drain. Discard the stalks and slice the caps. Dust the fish in half cornflour and shake off any excess. Heat the oil and deep-fry the fish for about 12 minutes until cooked. Drain on kitchen paper and keep warm.

Heat the oil and stir-fry the mushrooms, bamboo shoots, water chestnuts and cabbage for 3 minutes. Add the ginger, wine or sherry, 15 ml/1 tbsp of water, the soy sauce and sugar and stir-fry for 1 minute. Add the stock, salt and pepper, bring to the boil, cover and simmer for 3 minutes. Mix the cornflour with the remaining water, stir it into the pan and simmer, stirring, until the sauce thickens. Arrange the lettuce on a serving plate and place the fish on top. Pour over the vegetables and sauce and serve garnished with parsley.

Baked Whole Fish

Serves 4

1 large bass or similar fish

45 ml/3 tbsp cornflour (cornstarch)

45 ml/3 tbsp groundnut (peanut) oil

1 onion, chopped

2 cloves garlic, crushed

50 g/2 oz ham, cut into strips

100 g/4 oz peeled prawns

15 ml/1 tbsp soy sauce

15 ml/1 tbsp rice wine or dry sherry

5 ml/1 tsp sugar

5 ml/1 tsp salt

Coat the fish with cornflour. Heat the oil and fry the onion and garlic until lightly browned. Add the fish and fry until golden brown on both sides. Transfer the fish to a sheet of foil in a roasting tin and top with ham and prawns. Add the soy sauce, wine or sherry, sugar and salt to the pan and stir together well. Pour over the fish, close the foil over the top and bake in a preheated oven at 150¬∞C/ 300¬∞F/gas mark 2 for 20 minutes.

Braised Soy Fish

Serves 4

1 large bass or similar fish

salt

50 g/2 oz/¬Ω cup plain (all-purpose) flour

60 ml/4 tbsp groundnut (peanut) oil

3 slices ginger root, minced

3 spring onions (scallions), minced

250 ml/8 fl oz/1 cup water

45 ml/3 tbsp soy sauce

15 ml/1 tbsp rice wine or dry sherry

2.5 ml/¬Ω tsp sugar

Clean and scale the fish and score it diagonally on both sides. Sprinkle with salt and leave to stand for 10 minutes. Heat the oil and fry the fish until browned on both sides, turning once and basting with oil as you cook. Add the ginger, spring onions, water, soy sauce, wine or sherry and sugar, bring to the boil, cover and simmer for 20 minutes until the fish is cooked. Serve hot or cold.

Soy Fish with Oyster Sauce

Serves 4

1 large bass or similar fish

salt

60 ml/4 tbsp groundnut (peanut) oil

3 spring onions (scallions), minced

2 slices ginger root, minced

1 clove garlic, crushed

45 ml/3 tbsp oyster sauce

30 ml/2 tbsp soy sauce

5 ml/1 tsp sugar

250 ml/8 fl oz/1 cup fish stock

Clean and scale the fish and score diagonally a few times on each side. Sprinkle with salt and leave to stand for 10 minutes. Heat most of the oil and fry the fish until browned on both sides, turning once. Meanwhile, heat the remaining oil in a separate pan and fry the spring onions, ginger and garlic until lightly browned. Add the oyster sauce, soy sauce and sugar and stir-fry for 1 minute. Add the stock and bring to the boil. Pour the mixture into the browned fish, return to the boil, cover and simmer for about

15 minutes until the fish is cooked, turning once or twice during cooking.

Steamed Bass

Serves 4

1 large bass or similar fish
2.25 1/4 pts/10 cups water
3 slices ginger root, minced
15 ml/1 tbsp salt
15 ml/1 tbsp rice wine or dry sherry
30 ml/2 tbsp groundnut (peanut) oil

Clean and scale the fish and score both sides diagonally several times. Bring the water to a rolling boil in a large pan and add the remaining ingredients. Lower the fish into the water, cover tightly, turn off the heat and leave to stand for 30 minutes until the fish is cooked.

Braised Fish with Mushrooms

Serves 4

4 dried Chinese mushrooms

1 large carp or similar fish

salt

45 ml/3 tbsp groundnut (peanut) oil

2 spring onions (scallions), minced

1 slice ginger root, minced

3 cloves garlic, crushed

100 g/4 oz bamboo shoots, cut into strips

250 ml/8 fl oz/1 cup fish stock

30 ml/2 tbsp soy sauce

15 ml/1 tbsp rice wine or dry sherry

2.5 ml/¬Ω tsp sugar

Soak the mushrooms in warm water for 30 minutes then drain. Discard the stalks and slice the caps. Score the fish diagonally a few times on both sides, sprinkle with salt and leave to stand for 10 minutes. Heat the oil and fry the fish until lightly browned on both sides. Add the spring onions, ginger and garlic and fry for 2 minutes. Add the remaining ingredients, bring to the boil, cover and simmer for 15 minutes until the fish is cooked, turning once or twice and stirring occasionally.

Sweet and Sour Fish

Serves 4

1 large bass or similar fish

1 egg, beaten

50 g/2 oz cornflour (cornstarch)

oil for frying

For the sauce:

15 ml/1 tbsp groundnut (peanut) oil

1 green pepper, cut into strips

100 g/4 oz canned pineapple chunks in syrup

1 onion, cut into wedges

100 g/4 oz/¬Ω cup brown sugar

60 ml/4 tbsp chicken stock

60 ml/4 tbsp wine vinegar

15 ml/1 tbsp tomato pur√©e (paste)

15 ml/1 tbsp cornflour (cornstarch)

15 ml/1 tbsp soy sauce

3 spring onions (scallions), chopped

Clean the fish and remove the fins and head if you prefer. Coat it in beaten egg then in cornflour. Heat the oil and fry the fish until cooked through. Drain well and keep warm.

To make the sauce, heat the oil and fry the pepper, drained pineapple and onion for 4 minutes. Add 30 ml/2 tbsp of the pineapple syrup, the sugar, stock, wine vinegar, tomato purée, cornflour and soy sauce and bring to the boil, stirring. Simmer, stirring, until the sauce clears and thickens. Pour over the fish and serve sprinkled with spring onions.

Pork-Stuffed Fish

Serves 4

1 large carp or similar fish

salt

100 g/4 oz minced (ground) pork

1 spring onion (scallion), minced

4 slices ginger root, minced

15 ml/1 tbsp cornflour (cornstarch)

60 ml/4 tbsp soy sauce

15 ml/1 tbsp rice wine or dry sherry

5 ml/1 tsp sugar

75 ml/5 tbsp groundnut (peanut) oil

2 cloves garlic, crushed

1 onion, sliced

300 ml/¬Ω pt/1¬° cups water

Clean and scale the fish and sprinkle with salt. Mix the pork, spring onion, a little of the ginger, the cornflour, 15 ml/1 tbsp of soy sauce, the wine or sherry and sugar and use to stuff the fish. Heat the oil and fry the fish until lightly browned on both sides then remove it from the pan and drain off most of the oil. Add the garlic and remaining ginger and stir-fry until lightly browned.

Add the remaining soy sauce and the water, bring to the boil and simmer for 2 minutes. Return the fish to the pan, cover and simmer for about 30 minutes until the fish is cooked, turning once or twice.

Braised Spiced Carp

Serves 4

1 large carp or similar fish

150 ml/¬° pt/generous ¬Ω cup groundnut (peanut) oil

15 ml/1 tbsp sugar

2 cloves garlic, finely chopped

100 g/4 oz bamboo shoots, sliced

150 ml/¬° pt/generous ¬Ω cup fish stock

15 ml/1 tbsp rice wine or dry sherry

15 ml/1 tbsp soy sauce

2 spring onions (scallions), chopped

1 slice ginger root, chopped

15 ml/1 tbsp wine vinegar salt

Clean and scale the fish and soak it for several hours in cold water. Drain and pat dry then score each side several times. Heat the oil and fry the fish on both sides until firm. Remove from the pan and pour off and reserve all but 30 ml/2 tbsp of the oil. Add the sugar to the pan and stir until it darkens. Add the garlic and bamboo shoots and stir well. Add the remaining ingredients, bring to the boil, then return the fish to the pan, cover and simmer gently for about 15 minutes until the fish is cooked.

Place the fish on a warmed serving plate and strain the sauce over the top.

CPSIA information can be obtained
at www.ICGtesting.com
Printed in the USA
BVHW081243010421
603931BV00008B/536